STORIES FROM THE ENGLISH SAINTS

JOHN RICHARDSON

Stories from the English Saints

Foreword by
Cardinal Basil Hume OSB

ST PAULS

Illustrations by
Carole Benton (pp. 19, 36, 55, 73, 93, 110)
Andrew Gray (pp. 26, 50, 60, 87, 102, 123)

ST PAULS
Middlegreen, Slough SL3 6BT, United Kingdom
Moyglare Road, Maynooth, Co. Kildare, Ireland

© ST PAULS 1994

ISBN 085439 455 9

Printed by The Guernsey Press Co. Ltd, Guernsey, C.I.

ST PAULS is an activity of the priests and brothers of the
Society of St Paul who proclaim the Gospel through the media
of social communication

Contents

Foreword

Holy people, men and women, are always an ispiration. That is why the lives of the saints are so very important. A serious life of prayer must always involve some spiritual reading. The Bible, and especially the Gospels, have obvious claims on our attention. So do the lives of the saints.

Well-written lives of saints show us how holy men and women have translated the ideals and values of the Gospel into their lives. This book entitled "Stories from the English Saints", will help many people, and especially young persons, to explore the truths and values of the Gospel as they have been lived in practice.

Our island is rich in saints. For my part, I have always found great inspiration from the stories of the saints in Anglo-Saxon England, as told by the Venerable Bede, and from the lives of the martyrs who died for their faith in penal times.

I trust that this little book will give pleasure to many who may, through it, discover not only an inspiration for their lives but something about the rich heritage of saints in our land.

Cardinal Basil Hume OSB
Archbishop of Westminster

Introduction

All kinds of people have become saints. There have been king saints and beggar saints; mothers, nuns and girls; famous writers and people who could not read. This book tells the lives of only twelve of them. But even here, we have a soldier, a carpenter, a housewife, a lawyer, a princess, a herdsman and several priests and monks.

The differences between them were not only those of wealth or work. They were also different in character. Anselm was always gentle, even when violent men bullied him and shouted at him. Thomas Becket, on the other hand, had a fiery temper. Before his death, he argued with his murderers, and pushed one of them away.

Some, like Thomas More, loved to laugh and joke. Others, like Boniface, were usually more serious. Some, like Alban, went to their deaths without hesitation. Others, like Augustine and his monks, were frightened and only learnt to be brave through experience.

So there are all kinds of differences between the saints. But even so, all of them had one thing in common. They knew that the most important thing is to serve God. Some learnt it early and some late.

Dismas, who is not in this book, learnt it just before he died. He was one of the thieves who was crucified next to Jesus. The other thief cursed Jesus, but Dismas told him to stop and to fear God. Then, he asked Jesus to remember him when he came into his kingdom. And Jesus promised that they would be together that day in heaven.

Like Dismas, Alban learnt his lesson late. He was brought up to worship the Roman gods, and to think of Christianity as a bad religion. Thomas Becket was brought up a Christian, but for the first part of his life, he mostly cared about rich clothes and food. Only when he became archbishop did he change. Others learnt earlier, but the lesson for all was the same – to follow Jesus and serve God. And because they learnt it so well they became saints.

The saints in this book are English saints. That does not mean that they were all English people, or even that they lived most of their lives in England. Augustine and Anselm were Italians; Aidan came from Ireland. And Boniface, an Englishman, left his country in order to be a missionary in Germany.

But all had something to do with England. And all worked hard for Christianity in this country.

There are saints in the history of every country. Those of one are no better than those of another. We can learn from all how different kinds of people have lived holy lives. But the saints of our own country can sometimes be special to us. We remember them warmly because they are in some way connected with us.

They are part of our history, and helped make the country what it is. And they lived in the same places as we do, with the same ground under their feet and the same air around them. This means that we can imagine them more clearly than others – how they lived and what they were like.

But we do not remember holy men and women only because of what they were hundreds of years ago. It is also important to think of them because of what they are now. They are no longer people on earth like us, as they once were. They are now saints in heaven with God.

It is because of this that we pray to them. We do not worship them as we worship God. Instead, we speak to them and ask them to help us in our prayers by praying with us. We end the "Hail Mary" by asking Mary to "pray for us sinners, now and at the hour of our death". We can ask all the saints to do the same, to pray for us and our families and our countries. They are in heaven close to God, and their prayers can only make ours stronger.

Alban

As the gates of the cage creaked open, the crowd fell silent. It was the same before every event, the same tense waiting for death. Already that afternoon, they had watched several gladiators fight to the finish in the open space at the middle of the amphitheatre. Now it was time for the hunt.

The advertisements had promised a hunt between wild animals from Africa and condemned criminals. The criminals would not be armed as they often were. But these were criminals of a special kind. They were Christians.

When the gates were fully open, nothing happened for a few moments. Finally, one by one, the lions slunk warily out into the open space. It was always like this at first. The animals would keep to the shadows of the high walls which circled the central arena. The crowd would get restless and start to shout. Then, driven by hunger and by the blows of their keepers, the animals would turn on their prey.

On this afternoon, there were twelve victims – both men and women. When the gates had started to open they had embraced each other. Now, they knelt together in the middle of the arena, praying and waiting for death.

Some members of the crowd began to shout insults at the Christians, and encouragement at the animals. But not everyone reacted in that way. One young man sat in silence and watched curiously.

He found the whole thing hard to understand. These Christians certainly were a strange lot. In many ways, they were probably good enough people, and even good Roman citizens some of them. The rumours said they were honest and fair, and that they kept the empire's laws.

But in other ways, they were strange and not like true Romans at all. The advertisements had declared that two of those to be killed on this day were citizens from wealthy families. The others were slaves. But they all knelt there together in the sand. And they had all embraced, more like brothers and sisters than masters and slaves.

It was the same as that other strange thing you heard about the Christians, the way they forgave. There were stories of them forgiving their executioners and the men who sentenced them to death. Ordinary people cursed their killers. It was natural to seek revenge. Even the gods tried to punish those who wronged them.

But these Christians were different. It seemed almost a rule with them to bless their tormentors.

By now, things were starting to happen in the arena. Urged on by the cries of the crowd, the keepers had begun to prod at the lions with long spears from the safety of high walls. One large male lion suddenly roared, lashed at a spear, and moved towards the Christians. More of the crowd started to shout, caught in the excitement of noise and violence. The young man did not join them. He remained quiet and curious, watching these strange people in the middle of the arena.

Strangest of all was the fact that they did not have to be there. All they needed to do was to agree to worship the emperor, and to burn incense on an altar in front of his statue. If they did that, they would be released. It seemed simple enough.

Of course, some were so frightened by their arrest and the idea of execution that they did as they were asked. There were always tales of that happening. But others were more stubborn, and chose to die rather than worship the emperor and the Roman gods. And still their religion did not die out. In fact, if the gossip was true, there were more Christians in the empire now than ever.

By this time, most of the lions had moved away from the walls at the edge of the ring. One of the Christians stood up and raised his hands. It was impossible to tell what the gesture meant. He seemed to be holding his arms out towards the crowd, who were now shouting loudly for the lions to attack. Perhaps this was the blessing that people talked about. Perhaps it was the forgiveness.

The movement seemed to anger the leader of the lions, the large male. A sudden leap and he was on the man. With the crowd cheering from all sides, the killing began.

For more than two hundred years after the death of Christ, scenes like this were common throughout the Roman empire. There were periods when the Christians were left in peace. But at other periods, the authorities tried to destroy the new religion, by seeking out those who followed it. Usually these early Christians were given the chance of escape if they would worship the emperor. Those who refused were executed, often in public.

Among the crowds who watched these executions, many were excited by the shouting, the spectacle and the cruelty. Others must have been puzzled by the Christians – like the young man. Some must later have joined them.

Most of the names of those who died in the first centuries of Christianity are now forgotten. But many are still remembered, among them that of Alban.

He was a Roman soldier, stationed in England in a town called Verulamium. For most of his life, he was loyal to everything Roman, worshipping the emperor, like every good Roman, and also sacrificing to the other Roman gods – Jupiter, Mars, and Mercury.

As well as this official religion, he knew of different kinds of worship. He had met astrologers who said they could tell his fortune, and magicians who said they could improve it. Some of his friends in the army belonged to the tough, manly cult of Mithras. To follow this god, they had to endure pain, and push their bodies to the limits. Sometimes he heard tales of other sects – strange, secret groups, which claimed to know everything. Rumours of their wild ceremonies were always going round, but little was known for certain.

And then there were the Christians. They were another strange group, but strange in a different way. They chose to die rather than give up their God, and they went to death with a peculiar willingness.

It was not always easy to find out about them either. But perhaps Alban witnessed the deaths of some, and like the young man at the amphitheatre, was puzzled by the way they died. Later, he had the opportunity to learn more when, by chance, a Christian priest stayed with him as his guest.

Something about the priest impressed him. He was gentle when he talked and interested when he listened. But other people had those qualities, and this man was different from them. The difference was that his gentleness seemed to come from another life. He led a life apart from the ordinary life of eating and working and talking.

Alban watched this other life. He watched the priest going off to be alone, and praying night and day. This was something new to Alban, the way that the priest's mind was always on his God.

Eventually, the soldier began to question his guest about his religion. The Roman gods were like men – angry, greedy, unable to change fate. But this priest's God was different. He had made everything and he was a God of love.

Alban was convinced by what he learnt, and he asked the priest to baptise him. He did not, however, live long as a Christian. Someone informed the local judge that there was a priest in the house, and soldiers arrived to make a search. The priest was ready to give himself up, but Alban would hear nothing of that.

"I will go," he insisted. "You can do more good than I can. Quickly – let us change clothes."

Finding Alban dressed like a priest, the soldiers tied him up, and dragged him before the judge. They soon realised that they had been tricked.

"Do not think," the judge said angrily, "that you are safe. You have hidden a Christian priest. For this you will suffer all the punishment due to him. And who are you?"

"A Christian," Alban replied.

"Your name!" snapped the judge.

"I am called Alban. And I worship the living God who created all things."

With a bark of command, the judge ordered Alban to be dragged before the altars of the Roman gods.

*Finding Alban dressed like a priest, the soldiers tied him up,
and dragged him before the judge...*

"Sacrifice to these gods," he demanded.

"These are not gods," Alban answered. "They are nothing. And I will not leave the true God."

This answer only angered the judge more. He told the soldiers to take Alban away and beat him. Perhaps that would make him change his mind.

The new Christian was whipped and tortured, but he would not give up his faith. Finally, the judge ordered his execution.

Alban was led by the soldiers out of the town to the amphitheatre where he was to die. A great crowd watched him pass, and saw the quiet, gentle way in which he went to his death. Among the crowd was the man who had been given the job of executioner.

When Alban reached the arena, the man approached, threw down his sword and knelt at Alban's feet.

"What is the meaning of this?" the judge snarled.

"Let me die instead of this holy man," said the executioner.

"No," the judge spat back.

The executioner looked up at his intended victim.

"In that case," he said, "I will die with him."

A different man was ordered to carry out the sentence. He lifted the sword, and struck off the heads of Alban and his new companion.

But the death of someone like Alban is not the

end of his story. The judge who had ordered him killed was troubled by what he had done and by the way that Alban had died. For days he worried and thought. Finally, he commanded that the seeking out and killing of Christians must stop.

So it was throughout the Roman empire. The Christians would be hunted down, then the killing would stop, begin again, stop again. But all the time, their numbers grew. Eventually, Christianity replaced the old worship of gods and emperors as the religion of the empire. At that time, England too became, for a while, a Christian country.

Saint Alban was the first martyr of England, and the town of Verulamium where he lived and died is now called St. Albans after him. His feast day is 20th June.

Augustine

The forty monks sat silently on the benches round the long, dark hall, and waited. Their leader should be there soon. He had returned from his journey to Rome that morning, and told them all to assemble in the hall. He was going to give them Pope Gregory's answer to their request.

The little monk by the open door turned and glanced out of it. They had been away from Rome for several months now, and he longed to get back. Even here, in France, things were bad enough. The people were peasant farmers who spoke a strange language and followed strange customs. There were no paved streets, no fine buildings, no cities and few books. All this made it hard to lead the life of prayer and study which he had known in Rome.

But at least the people here were Christians. In England, where the monks were going, they were heathens, who worshipped false gods with bloody sacrifices. The place had been Christian once, of course. Saint Alban had died there 300 years ago, and later, the country had been converted. But then, the fierce English invaders had come, and had driven the Christians into the hills. Now these savages ruled the island.

The little monk glanced out of the door a second time.

He had heard terrible tales about the English since he had left Rome. They were so primitive, it seemed, that they had no proper buildings, but lived in wooden shacks, where they cooked and ate and slept. They did not read or write or study or pray. All their energy went into their farms and their feuds.

There had been much talk of these feuds. The English were, it was said, always fighting and killing because of insults or injuries done to brothers or cousins or uncles. It was their rule of honour that every death had to be repaid with another death. So, the feuds went on for years and years as families and tribes tried to even the score. And after every murder and every battle, so the rumour went, the victors would return to their huts and feast and drink, and boast and sing about the killing.

The little monk shuddered. He, like his companions, had no heart for this journey. How could they convert such a wild, savage race? And without even knowing their language?

Once more he glanced out of the door.

There was little chance that they would be allowed to return as they had asked. It was Gregory himself, once their beloved abbot and now the pope, who had sent them on this mission. Everyone knew the story of what had first moved him to it. Impressed by the beauty of some slaves in the market in Rome, he had asked the trader what kind of people they were.

"Angles," the man had replied. "Fierce pagans from the island of Britain."

"They are well named," Gregory had replied. "For they are like angels from heaven."

After that, he could not forget these Angles – or angels as he had called them. Unhappy that such beautiful people were pagans; he had planned to visit them himself, and try to convert them to Christianity. But he had been made pope, and now he could not leave Rome. So, instead someone else had to do the job – Augustine and his forty monks!

Finding that he was thinking angrily of Gregory, the little monk stopped himself, silently repeated a prayer to himself the sign of the cross. It was just that he longed to return to Rome.

The hall darkened as a figure appeared in the doorway. It was Augustine. The monks, their hearts beating, watched him take his place at the centre of the room. Having greeted them and said a prayer, he produced a scroll from his black habit.

"Our holy father has replied to your request," he said, and began to read.

"It is better never to start a good work than to start one and leave it unfinished. Therefore, you must continue. Do not let rumours and gossip stop you. But finish the holy task that God has set you

25

"*Our holy father has replied to your request,*" he said,
and began to read.

on. Obey Augustine in all things, for obedience is good for your souls. God keep you in safety, my most beloved sons."

Augustine lifted his head from his reading and gravely regarded the monks on the benches round him.

"So, brothers, we must go on," he said at last.

The little monk looked up. For weeks he had been hoping that the pope would agree to their request, that they would be allowed to return to Rome. Now the hope was gone. He and his fellow monks had to push on through this savage France to that even more savage England.

He had expected that such an answer would bring misery to him. But the strange thing was that this did not happen. As he looked at his brothers in the dim hall, he suddenly felt a great happiness come over him. At last his mind had changed – he wanted to travel to England and help convert the fierce English.

They landed a few weeks later at Thanet, an island of the kingdom of Kent. Since none of them could speak English, they had brought interpreters from France. One of these was sent with a message to Ethelbert, the king. Augustine hoped that Ethelbert might welcome them because he had a Christian wife.

When the reply came, it told them to remain on the island and wait. Some days later the king arrived. He commanded his servants to set out seats, benches, spears and banners in the open air.

"The spells of magicians work best under a roof," he said. "We can avoid their magic by avoiding being indoors with them. In that way, they will not be able to harm us."

When the preparations were made, he ordered the monks to be brought before him. They approached in procession, dressed in their black habits. At the front, one carried a silver crucifix on a pole, and another carried a picture of Jesus.

As they approached they chanted in Latin. It was a quiet and gentle music, different from anything the king and his followers had ever known. When the chanting stopped, the king told Augustine to sit and tell of his religion. Speaking through an interpreter, Augustine explained that theirs was a religion of peace and love, and that it offered the hope of everlasting life.

"Your words are good," said the king when Augustine had finished speaking. "But what you say is new and strange to me, and I cannot give up the English customs which I have always followed. Even so, you have come a long way in the hope of helping us. For this reason, I will allow you to stay here. My people will leave you in peace and give you food. And you may preach to them, and win some, if you can, for your religion."

Soon after this meeting the monks moved to Canterbury. There, they settled down to lives of worship like those they had led in Rome. They fasted and prayed and celebrated Mass. They had no possessions of their own, and they took from their English hosts only enough food to live.

In one way, though, their lives were different from what they had been in Rome. Here, they had to spend more time in teaching people about Christianity. Using interpreters, they would go among the English and preach, slowly telling them more about their religion.

But people did not only learn from their preaching. They also learnt from seeing the way they lived, from their simplicity and holiness. And in England Augustine discovered that he had a gift for healing the sick. His cures impressed those who saw them or heard of them.

Through this work, the monks soon found that the English were not as bad as the rumours in France had said. It was true that their buildings were very rough, that they were heathens, and that they spent a lot of energy on their feuds and quarrels. But their king had welcomed the monks generously, and many of his people were also kind to them.

Gradually, the monks began to make converts. The king himself was baptised, and with him, many of his people. More and more followed as word spread of the new religion, and of Augustine's cure. From Rome Pope Gregory who had sent the monks to England watched their success with happiness. When he learnt of the baptisms, he sent out more monks and priests to help with the work.

He was always ready to give Augustine advice about his difficult task. There were many problems. One of the worst was how to deal with the old heathen worship of the English, with its temples and festivals. Gregory's advice about this, like his advice about everything, was generous as wise.

Do not destroy what does not need to be destroyed, he said. People should keep their old customs as long as they are not against God. Temples should not be pulled down, but should be made into churches. And heathen festivals should be made into Christian festivals.

And so, following the teaching of Gregory, Augustine was able to begin spreading Christianity among the English. Sometimes the converts would lose heart when things went badly, or would want to go back to the old ways of magic and sacrifice, or would simply forget their new religion in the daily work of farming. But slowly, the Christian faith took root in their minds and hearts.

Augustine died in 604, only seven years after his arrival in England. In the same year Pope Gregory also died, a man of such wisdom that today we call him Gregory the Great.

There were still many problems ahead for English Christianity. There were wars with heathen kings, and later, raids by heathen vikings. There were even fierce quarrels with the first Christians of the island, those who had fled into the mountains when the English invaded.

But ever since Augustine's monks landed in Thanet, Christianity has belonged to England. It is for this reason that he, and his master Gregory, are known as the Apostles of the English.

Augustine's feast is on 27th May; Gregory's on 3rd September.

Aidan

A bell was ringing in the little group of stone buildings, calling the elders to a meeting. All over the island of Iona they got up from their work. One put down his pen and another laid aside his hoe. A third rose from his prayers, and a fourth handed the fishing net he had been mending to his brother monks. Others still abandoned hammer or book or water bucket or mixing bowl in order to answer the bell.

Soon they could be seen moving along the paths to the buildings. They wore dark habits, and the cold Scottish winds coming in from the sea ruffled their clothes as they walked.

It was an important meeting. One of the monks, a popular man in the monastery, had just returned from Northumbria in the north of England. He had gone to take Christianity to the people there, and now he had to explain the failure of his mission.

When they had all gathered in the long meeting room, the abbot led them in prayer. Then the monk spoke, sadly and for a long time, about the country he had just visited. Aidan, sitting among the others, listened carefully to what he said.

"They are always fighting," the monk finished.

"If they're not fighting other heathen tribes, they're fighting among themselves." He sighed. "I could teach them nothing."

"But it was their own king, Oswald," the abbot said gently, "who asked you to go. Oswald, our brother who once lived among us. He wants his people to be Christian like himself."

"He lived among us, Father," the monk answered, "because he was escaping a war in his own country. Their minds are full of battles and blood. They are not ready for the message of peace."

There was a silence before the abbot spoke again.

"But we learn that there are now many Christians among the English in the south of the country. Our brothers from Rome have had great success there. And one of them, Paulinus, has even made converts in the north."

The monk stared gloomily ahead of him.

"I heard of Paulinus when I was there. But he has now gone back to the south. And with good reason. These people do not want to be Christians. They could understand nothing of what I told them."

At this point Aidan, who had been following the conversation closely, decided to speak.

"Perhaps, brother," he said, "you tried to teach too much, and too soon. These are simple people, who must be given easy lessons at first. They can only be led slowly to knowledge of God."

The monk admitted that this could be so, and the discussion went on. Finally, it was decided to try a second mission to the north of England. This time, the mission would be led by Aidan. He would be abbot of the brothers who went with him, and would become bishop of Northumbria.

When Aidan arrived there, he was met by King Oswald. The king allowed him to choose where he would build his church and monastery. He chose the island of Lindisfarne, which can only be reached from the coast at low tide. It was a cold, wild place, buffeted by wind and rain from the sea.

But colder and wilder still were the islands out in the sea beyond Lindisfarne. Later, it became Aidan's habit to go to one of these during Lent, or when he needed time for thought. On the windy rock, alone except for the sea birds and seals, he could pray with all his soul.

Aidan began the work of conversion as soon as he arrived in Northumbria. King Oswald wanted the teaching to start with his own followers. But Aidan, an Irishman, knew very little English, and none of his monks knew any more than he. There was only one solution. Aidan must preach, while Oswald, the king, acted as humble interpreter.

Later, when Aidan had learnt to speak English, he travelled about Northumbria, teaching every-one he met about his religion. He went on foot,

The king allowed him to choose where he would build his church and monastery.

ate only the simplest food, and avoided the mistake of the monk who had gone before him. He did not tell the Northumbrians about the mysteries of Christianity, but began with the simple things – the way that God created the world, the birth of Jesus, his teaching of love.

In all his work Aidan had the help of Oswald, who was himself a good Christian. One Easter Sunday, the king held a great feast. It was his custom to give something to the poor at such times, and he ordered his steward to do this. But the steward soon came back to say that the food he had put aside was not enough. Many more poor people were outside, hoping to be given something.

The king looked at the table laden with many kinds of meat.

"Take all this," he said to the steward. He lifted the large silver dish that was in front of him. "And melt this down, to divide among them."

Aidan touched the king's hand and prayed.

"May this arm never perish."

Oswald did not live long after that. His enemy, Penda, a heathen king, defeated him in battle, and had his body broken up as an offering to Woden, god of war. Only the arm that Aidan had touched stayed whole.

The new king of Northumbria was called Oswin. He was a cousin of Oswald's, and like him, was eager to help Aidan in his work. The best way to do this, he thought, was to give the bishop a fine horse. The gift would allow Aidan to travel more easily round Northumbria to tell the people about Christianity.

Aidan, however, was not the man to keep such a horse. Soon after receiving it, he gave it away, with saddle and bridle, to a beggar he met by the roadside.

When King Oswin learnt of this he was very angry. It seemed to him that Aidan had not shown proper gratitude for the gift. They met one evening before dinner, when the king had just returned, tired, from hunting.

"Why did you give that horse to a poor man?" he asked angrily. "It was a royal horse picked out for you by me. Why did you scorn my gift?"

"Is a horse more valuable to you than the Son of God?" Aidan answered gently.

The king turned his back, and stamped over to the fire. He stood there for a few moments staring gloomily into the flames. Suddenly he tugged off his sword, and went quickly to the place where Aidan had sat down. He knelt before him.

"Forgive me," he said. "I will never mention this again. And I will never check how much money you give to the children of God."

Aidan took Oswin's arm and lifted him up.

"I forgive your anger," he answered. "But you must sit down to your meal and forget your sad thoughts."

Although the people of Northumbria had a holy

bishop and a holy king, they did not have peace. There were constant fights and battles. Sometimes the heathen Penda would attack, and sometimes there would be skirmishes between Oswin's men and those of his cousin who ruled a neighbouring kingdom.

One of Penda's raids reached as far as the royal town of Bamburgh. There he was stopped. The town consisted of the king's palace, a large wooden hall, and the many wooden huts built round it. These were perched for defence on a high rock next to the sea.

The heathen king and his men first tried to charge the rock, but they were beaten back. Then Penda ordered his army to make camp, in the hope that they could starve the Northumbrians out. But the people of the town were well prepared, so this plan failed as well.

Finally, Penda decided to try something else. He ordered a few of his best men to creep up to the outer huts and set fire to them. The flames licked at the dry wood and curled into the thatch. A wind sprang up. Sparks flew from one hut to the next. Soon the whole town would be on fire. Penda's men gathered near the burning huts, ready to slaughter those who came running out of the flames.

Bamburgh was only a few miles south of Aidan's church in Lindisfarne. But Aidan was not at Lindisfarne at the time of the raid. He had gone off alone to pray at the little island out in the sea. From the island, he could see across the waves to the coast. A black trail of smoke rose from the town on the rock, high into the sky. Aidan fell onto his knees.

"Lord," he cried. "See what evil Penda does."

As Aidan spoke the winds changed. The flames which had been threatening to destroy the town turned instead towards Penda's men. The fire burnt their clothes, and fear chilled their hearts. They turned and ran back to their camp, where they quickly packed and left.

Oswin was to die soon afterwords. The argument with his cousin grew into a war, and Oswin found himself with his men facing his cousin's army. Since being a child, he had heard tales of fights and wars, of great deeds and many deaths. He had sometimes fought himself, and he had listened to songs of battle during the feasts in royal halls.

But fighting and killing were not part of the religion which he had tried to live in his life and to spread in his kingdom. His army was sure to lose, and he had no heart for more bloodshed. He turned to his men and told them to go home.

With one trusted soldier, he travelled to the hall of his friend, Hunwald. But there are men who will betray anything in the hope of reward, and Hunwald was one of these. He sent word to the new king, soldiers arrived and Oswin was murdered. Later, the king was saddened by what he had done. He paid for a monastery to be built on the site of the murder. There, the monks could pray both for his soul and for that of Oswin.

It was not long after Oswin's death that Aidan also died. He was on one of his journeys round the countryside when he fell sick. The monks built him a little tent close to the wall of the church in Bamburgh. It was there that he passed peacefully away.

That was in the year 651. There were still many in Northumbria who were not Christians. Many more were Christians who cared little about their religion and knew less. But others had taken the faith into their hearts, and would continue the work which Aidan had started.

Aidan had succeeded where his brother monk from Iona had failed. He had planted Christianity in the north of England, just as Augustine had planted it in the south. His feast is on 31st August.

Hilda

Caedmon, the herdsman, held up the flickering flame of his lamp and looked round the stable. The horses were fed and comfortable. He bent down and brushed away some straw to make a clear patch on the muddy floor. There, where it could do no harm, he placed his lamp.

By the weak light, he knelt to pray. He knew only the few simple prayers which the monks had taught him. But he repeated these carefully, out of respect for the monks and their holy abbess Hilda, and out of love for God. When his prayers were finished, he made a place for himself in the straw, blew out the lamp, and pulled his blanket over him.

It was a stormy night. He could hear the wind blowing in the trees outside and could feel it through the thin wooden walls of the stables. From the distance he could also hear the sound of singing in the hall. The feast which he had left early was still going on.

The same thing had often happened before. Caedmon had been an unimportant guest at many other feasts in long, smoky halls. Everyone would eat and drink and talk. Then, later in the evening, the host would order the harp to be taken down from its place on the wall. It would be passed from person to person, and each in turn would take it and sing a song.

Some sang of battle, some of mighty deeds, some of great voyages. Only Caedmon did not sing. He could not. And when he saw the harp come down from the wall, he would quietly get up, leave the hall, and go to his bed. So it had been at this feast; so it had always been.

It was not long that evening before Caedmon was asleep, and soon afterwards, he was dreaming. In his dream, he saw a stranger coming towards him.

"Caedmon," the stranger said, "sing a song for me."

"I cannot sing," he answered. "That was why I left the feast and came to my bed."

But the stranger was not to be put off.

"Even so, you must sing," he insisted.

"What shall I sing?"

"The song of the creation of the world."

At this command, Caedmon immediately began to sing words which he had never heard before.

"Now we must praise the king of heaven," he sang, "praise his strength and his wisdom, praise the Lord eternal who made all things wonderful. He built for us the roof of heaven, Holy Creator; he built for us the things of the world, Protector of Men; he built for us the earth below, Master Al-mighty."

When Caedmon woke up next morning in the cold damp stable, he remembered his song of joy and began to add more to it.

That day, he went about his work with a new happiness, and later on, he told his master of the dream. The master, who knew the herdsman had never been a singer, was surprised, and he asked to hear the song. The beauty of the words and the music filled him with delight.

Close to the village where Caedmon and his master lived was the abbey of Whitby. The master decided to take Caedmon there so that the abbess and her monks could hear of the dream.

The poor herdsman was led into a great room in the abbey. Everything there was strange to him, the stone walls, the table of polished wood, the great books that lay on it. But strangest and most frightening of all were the people who sat round the table.

Caedmon had in the past spoken with some of the abbey's monks. Indeed, it was these monks who had taught him what little he knew about his religion. And he had sometimes seen the abbess, Hilda, passing in the distance. He knew she belonged to a royal family, and like all the people of those parts, he had heard what a good and holy woman she was. But he had never spoken with the abbess or with her priests, and now he was in the same room as them. Everyone was looking at Caedmon and waiting for him to speak.

He glanced round and wondered about them. What did they think of him with his ragged clothes and rough hands? A herdsman who could not even read? And what would they think when they heard of his dream? The dream of someone as ignorant as him?

Hilda saw his hesitation and smiled.

"Caedmon," she said, "please tell us your dream."

At once, his fear disappeared. He began to explain what he had dreamt, and when that was finished, to repeat his song. The men sitting round the table looked puzzled, and started to talk together in a language that Caedmon did not understand. At last, Hilda spoke again.

"We believe," she said, "that you have been given a great gift from God. But we must make a small test. One of the brothers will teach you something from the Bible, and we want you to go away and try to make a new song from that. Do you agree to such a test?"

Caedmon agreed happily, and returned the next day with his new song. Once again, it moved all those who heard it.

After that, at Hilda's invitation, he joined the abbey, where he was given a special task. The monks would explain parts of the Bible to him, and he would make songs from what he heard.

His songs were so lovely that they brought to Christianity many who were not yet Christians, and strengthened in it many who were.

It was Hilda's wisdom that gave Caedmon the chance to make his songs.

A lot of people used to come to her abbey for help and advice, among them kings and great men. These would arrive in a big crowd of horses, of servants with banners, and of soldiers with spears. But Hilda, the royal abbess, was not impressed by riches or power.

The way she organised her abbey showed this. All her monks and nuns had to lead the same simple lives, and among them there were no rich or poor, great or small. It was important, she thought, to see everyone as God's child. And because of this, she could recognise the gift given to a simple herdsman like Caedmon.

Hilda had been born a heathen princess of the fierce tribes of northern England. But even before her birth, there was a sign of the kind of woman she would become. Her parents were separated because of one of the many wars of those dark days. One night, her mother dreamt that she was looking everywhere for her husband, but she could not find him.

When at last she stopped looking, she noticed a jewel under her cloak. She took the jewel out and it shone so brightly that its light filled the whole country. Later, Hilda would shine in the darkness like that jewel.

She grew up among heathen temples and heathen festivals. Only now and then did she hear rumours of the new religion which had come to the south of the country. But when she was still a girl, a Christian queen arrived in the north. With the queen was a priest called Paulinus.

Slowly, the priest taught the people of the area about his religion. Some became convinced and some were baptised. Eventually, Hilda joined them, and was baptised with the king in a little wooden church at York.

She did not, however, become a nun straightaway. For many years, she continued the life of an English princess. At last, though, at the age of thirty-three, she took the advice of Bishop Aidan of Lindisfarne. She decided to devote her life to religion, became a sister, and then the abbess of Whitby.

The abbess had great power over her monks and nuns, but Hilda always used her power wisely. She encouraged her people to work, pray and study hard, so that later five of her monks became bishops. But other things were even more important than study. With Hilda's teaching and example, her abbey was a place of peace and kindness.

She spent her last years suffering from a painful disease. Throughout her sickness, she continued to see all those who came to her for advice and help, and she continued to praise God. At last her final day arrived. Just as dawn was breaking, she took communion and called together some of her monks and nuns.

"Keep peace among yourselves," she said. "And be at peace with others."

As she was speaking she died.

Strange things happened at the moment she died. One of the nuns in a convent some miles away was awoken by the sound of a bell. She looked up and saw the soul of Hilda going into heaven, surrounded by angels and light. The nun woke her sisters and they all prayed together until news of the death arrived.

Another nun in a separate part of Hilda's own convent woke to see the same vision. She, too, awakened those near her, to tell them the news and to ask them to pray for the soul of their abbess.

Hilda died in the year 680. She had lived at a time when England was slowly becoming a Christian country. Fighting and the worship of strange gods were all around. But when people heard of the new religion, and when they saw the holy lives in abbeys like Whitby, they began to give up the old ways.

Caedmon, a simple herdsman, became a monk and a poet. But Caedmon was not the only one. Many more flocked to lead Christian lives under the guidance of Hilda. A light shone from her like the light from the jewel in her mother's dream.

But it shone in a way that her mother could never have expected.

She is one of the great early English saints. Her feast is on 17th November.

Boniface

The great German forest seemed to go on forever. Everywhere you looked there were trees, and darkness under the trees. Trees and darkness, darkness and trees, going on to the ends of the earth. But it was what lived in the darkness that made you shiver. Who could know of all the witches and spirits and werewolves of that endless forest shade?

The famous oak stood in a small clearing. It was a huge tree and very old, but that was not the reason it was famous. Its fame came from its holiness, for this was Thor's oak, a tree sacred to the great thunder god of the German tribesmen.

On this day, many from the tribes had gathered near the god's oak to see how he would defend it. They were standing in small silent groups round the edges of the clearing, and waiting. The afternoon was very still, not a breath of wind stirring. Overhead, clouds were slowly gathering.

The people had known of Thor and of the tree since they had been children. They had made sacrifices to him and tried to keep him happy. All the spirits of the dark forest, all the witches and werewolves, had to be kept happy in the same way, with offerings and sacrifices. That was part of life – it always had been.

But now there was this new, foreign religion that spoke of peace and light. Many of those at the edge of the clearing had tried it for a year or two. Certainly, there was something lovely in its teaching, and people spoke of the power of its magic.

But it was hard to believe in peace and light in the shadow of the dark forest. No one knew if the foreign religion was true. But everyone knew that the forest was there – trees and darkness without end.

So most returned to the old ways of magic and sacrifice. Of course, some still went to the ceremonies of the new religion, hoping to keep the foreign god happy as well. And a few had even stayed faithful to him alone. It was because of them that the crowd was waiting in the forest now.

From the distance came the sound of chanting. The Christians were coming to make trial with Thor. People had talked of nothing else for weeks. When the foreign priest had come back from far away, those who had stayed with the new religion had gone to him. These Christian tribesmen had told tales of how others had returned to the old worship. And they had begged the priest to destroy the tree. He had brought some new power back with him, they said, and should use it at once.

At first, he had hesitated. Perhaps, he was afraid. That was certainly the rumour in the villages. His god might really be weaker than Thor. All the talk of peace and light might only be talk, and the Christians might be able to do nothing against the darkness of the forest.

But then the gossip had changed. The foreign priest had agreed to do what his followers had asked. He had promised to destroy the tree.

Many in the villages had laughed darkly when they heard this. The priest had promised, but perhaps he did not have the power to carry out his promise. Perhaps he would not destroy the tree, but rather, the great god, Thor, would destroy him. If it was to be a fight between the priest and the god of the dark forest, perhaps the god would win.

No one knew how he would win, but many had come prepared. Beneath the bright cloaks of the tribesmen hung swords and axes. Most expected their weapons to be in use before the end of the afternoon.

By now, it was growing quite late. The light had become dim under the gathering clouds and in the shadows of the trees. The atmosphere among the crowd was growing ever more tense as the chanting came closer.

At last, a new figure appeared in the clearing. It was one of the foreign monks, carrying their symbol, a cross set on a pole. The monk was followed by more dressed like him, and in the middle of them walked their leader, the priest. Behind the monks came the German Christians, quiet and worried. They knew of the rumours and of the swords as well as anyone. Perhaps they too expected the afternoon to end with blood.

The little procession, still chanting, approached the tree, came to a halt and fell silent. Their leader strode out of the group and held up his arms. For several moments, there was no sound in the clearing, and then he began to speak in a foreign language. The tribesmen at the edges knew what this meant. The priest was trying to cast a spell, to work some magic more powerful even than Thor's.

At length, he stopped, made a sign on his chest and gestured at one of his followers. The monk stepped forward and held out an axe. Without looking at the waiting Germans, the leader took it and approached the tree. Carefully, he set his feet apart and weighed the axe in his hands.

Everyone watched. Surely he would not try to destroy the huge tree by himself. But no one spoke or moved. Nothing broke the silence of the dusky clearing.

Then, he lifted the axe, and swung. There was a loud "chop" sound as the axe sank into the trunk. Nothing else happened. He pulled it free and swung a second time – again "chop" and nothing more.

Some of the men at the edge of the clearing muttered to each other. One reached beneath his cloak, and touched the handle of his sword.

Carefully, he set his feet apart and weighed the axe in his hands.

The priest was taking his third swing. A third "chop" rang out, but this time there was also a new noise – the noise of wind.

People all around were looking up. The branches of the tree which for hours had hung so still were now moving. Men pointed and talked urgently; more felt for their weapons. Only the priest seemed not to have noticed the wind. He continued to swing the axe.

But the wind was growing stronger. At a word from one of them, the monks began to chant. The sound of the axe continued. It was accompanied now by loud creaks of straining wood. Some of the men at the edge of the clearing were disappearing into the trees. The priest struck again. Another loud creak, and the tree leaned slowly away from the axe.

The people standing under the tree scattered, except for the little band of monks. The sound of the wind was growing ever stronger. The priest struck again – another creak, louder than any before.

The tree leaned further, and the priest stood back. Wind was still tugging at the branches, and slowly the great tree keeled over and fell with a crash to the ground. There, it broke into four huge pieces.

A shaft of sunlight lit the clearing. It was quiet once more, but no longer with the tense quiet of earlier. The monks, the only people left there, were silent for joy. Later, they would pray, return to their monastery and prepare themselves to receive all those who would come to learn of their religion.

The foreign priest who cut down the tree was an Englishman called Boniface. He had grown up in the England made by Augustine, Aidan, Hilda and their followers. There were still some heathens in the country, but Christianity was strong, and Boniface spent the first half of his life inside the peaceful walls of a monastery.

But often he longed for something else, and his thoughts turned towards Germany. Missionaries were already at work in parts of the country, and some had met success. Others worked alone, lost in the great dark forests, with few believers near them. To the north, things were even worse. The people knew nothing of Christianity, and instead of praying to God, they comforted themselves with magic.

Boniface was already nearly forty when he left his quiet life as a monk to become a missionary in Germany. He went first to Rome, to receive the blessing of the pope, and then began work in the forests. A few years later, he went to Rome again, this time to be made bishop. It was on his return that he cut down the great oak.

The event was a turning point in the district, but for Boniface there was still much work ahead. He wrote to England for supplies and help. From one abbey he asked for books, and from another, part of the Bible written out in gold letters. Beautiful things like this made a great impression on the people of the forest. But what he needed most of all were helpers. These came to him from monasteries and convents all over England, and some of them are still remembered today.

One was Lioba, an English nun and a relation of Boniface. After some preparation, she set off with four other nuns on the long journey to Germany. There, they started an abbey and a school. They taught children in the school, and they taught the local people through their holy lives.

The same was happening all over Germany. Abbeys were being set up by the rivers and in forest clearings. The Germans learnt of the new religion from the monks and nuns, and they saw it at work in their lives. Gradually, the old fear of forest and darkness began to grow smaller.

Boniface was busy in all this work. He helped and advised, and as he did so, he rose higher in the Church, until he was an archbishop. Always he used his power to spread faith among the German Christians.

By the end of his life, he had done a lot, and the Church in some parts of Germany was strong. But Boniface's mind kept going back to those heathen Germans of the north. Eventually, with the permission of the pope, he gave up his position of archbishop. He was nearly eighty, but this did not change his plan. He dressed himself again in the black habit of the monk, and set off with a few companions towards the north.

At first, they had success, making new converts and baptising them. Some wanted to be confirmed, and on Pentecost, Boniface and his companions pitched their tent in the little field where they were to meet. The great forest was all around, and Boniface sat in the tent and waited.

From outside, came the sounds of shouting and horses. Suddenly, one of the monks rushed in.

"There is a band of heathen warriors," he said. "They're threatening to kill us. Should we fight?"

Boniface glanced at the travelling chest which stood in the corner. In it was a book about holy death.

"No," he answered at last. "That would not be true to our faith. Come, let us go to them."

He led his followers out towards the band waiting in the shadow of the forest. There was no time to explain or bless. In a moment, the warriors were on them, and Boniface, with some of his friends, was dead on the grass.

Boniface died in the year 754. Although he was killed by violence and fear, he was not defeated by them. His work and his name lived after him. We celebrate his feast on 5th June.

*The young man, Dunstan, sat on a dry rock,
and gazed sadly out over the marshes.*

Dunstan

The young man, Dunstan, sat on a dry rock, and gazed sadly out over the marshes. It seemed to him that all glories were past glories. Everything worthwhile had happened long ago, and the present world was a small and petty place.

Away in the distance was the Island of Athelney. It was there that the great King Alfred had retreated sixty years ago. From the island, Alfred had ridden out to attack the invading vikings. Battle by battle he had beaten them back, until the kingdom had become English once more.

Alfred had been a great hero, but kings were not like that now. Dunstan knew they were not from what he had seen at the court of King Athelstan. Everyone there was busy trying to catch the king's eye, in the hope of becoming his favourite. The place was full of boasts and whispers and tales.

And the king listened to the lies that were told to him! So, when some of Dunstan's cousins had spread gossip about him, he had been sent away – banished from the court. That was why he now sat alone among the marshes.

The cousins had said he was a heathen, and that

he practised magic. They claimed to have heard him repeat spells, but they were wrong. The spells were only prayers. It was just that these cousins could not understand someone at the court who spent time praying. But then, they did not know that Dunstan was thinking of becoming a monk.

Above the marshes far away was a hill, and beneath the hill lay the old Abbey of Glastonbury. It was not the holy place it had once been. The buildings were in ruins, and the monks did not pray very often or very carefully. In fact it was difficult to say what the attraction of the abbey was. But even so, Dunstan had loved it since he had been a boy.

Once his father had taken him to hear the night prayers. The church was dark except for the light of candles. A strong smell of incense and old stone filled the air. There were not many monks, and some of those perhaps not very good, but they chanted beautifully.

Later in the night the little boy dreamt a strange dream. An old man, clothed in white, came to his bedside. He took his hand and showed him a beautiful new monastery, with many holy monks.

At another time, when Dunstan was sick, he walked in his sleep to the church. Still sleeping, he climbed a ladder onto the roof, then clambered down into the church. His parents found him there the next morning.

But the abbey now was like everything else. Its

glory was in the past. Two hundred years ago, England had sent countless monks and nuns to Germany to help Boniface in his work. But later, the vikings came to England with raiding parties or great armies. They killed the monks, burnt the abbeys, and stole their holy treasures.

The vikings had been driven back at last, and England was now an English country again. It was even a Christian country. But it had kings who listened to gossip, and abbeys which did not follow the Christian rule.

Dunstan sighed. And if you prayed, people believed you were a heathen. They believed your prayers were magic spells. It hardly seemed worth becoming a monk – just to live in a ruined abbey and have everyone think badly of you.

He stood up from his rock, and began to walk. The countryside was very marshy, and he had to pick his way carefully over streams and between bogs. In the distance was a group of trees on a piece of slightly higher ground. It was this hillock that Dunstan was heading for.

As he approached the trees, he saw a dark shape move among them. His heart began to beat faster. A voice called something, and was answered by laughter. There were people there in the trees' shade.

He was now very close, and he could see several figures moving in the dim light. A voice spoke encouragement, and a young man came out of the trees. Behind him appeared another, then another and another. Of course, Dunstan recognised them at once. They were his cousins, the ones who had told the king he was a heathen.

"A pleasant surprise," their leader said mockingly. The others laughed.

Dunstan ignored them and tried to push past. But the men were standing close together, blocking his path.

"Been casting your spells?" the leader went on. "Or making sacrifices?"

Dunstan remained silent.

"I asked a question," insisted the leader.

Again Dunstan said nothing, and again he tried to get past the men. One of them pushed him. He stumbled. A foot kicked at his legs, and before he could do anything, he was on the grass, with the men round him. They kicked and kicked – everywhere, at his legs, at his body, at his head.

At last they stopped, too tired to kick more. They tied his hands and legs together, threw him into the bog, and left. Dunstan lay in the cold mud, his whole body aching. After a while, he began to wriggle his hands free from their cords. It took some time, but eventually, he pulled them loose. Slowly, he dragged himself out of the bog.

On the bank, he touched his bruises gingerly. His feet were still tied, and he began to tug with his numb fingers at the knots. When they finally came undone, he was ready to set off. Covered in mud and very sore, he stumbled through the marshes in the direction of a friend's home.

As he approached the long low hall, the dogs ran out to him, barking furiously. One crouched snarling ready to spring. Almost too tired to stand, Dunstan managed to open his lips and speak. At the sound of his voice, the dogs immediately stopped their barking. They trotted up to him, and rubbed their bodies against his legs.

"It is sad," thought Dunstan, "that my cousins should turn on me like dogs, while these dogs can show a true human kindness."

Dunstan was ill for a long time after that. In his illness he thought a lot about what to do with his life. He wanted to become a monk, but there were many reasons why he should not. People were urging him to marry and to live a life at court. The abbeys were not the holy places he longed for. And was it worth being a monk in a world full of people like his cousins?

In the end, Dunstan put all these doubts aside. No good cursing his cousins, he thought – better to lead a good life himself. And no good complaining about the abbeys – better to do something to improve them. So, he took a small cell at Glastonbury. There, he spent his time praying, painting and studying.

But he was not left alone at the abbey for long. A new king, Edmund, came to the throne. He needed advice and he sent for Dunstan to help him. Once again, though, the gossip and the rumours started. People told lies about Dunstan. The king believed them, spoke angrily to the monk, and sent him out of his presence.

Not long afterwards, Edmund went out hunting with his nobles. They took a pack of hounds and rode after deer. Soon a stag was spotted and they gave chase. As they galloped over moors and through woods, the king was somehow separated from the rest of the party. But it was a magnificent stag he was chasing, and he rode on after it. For miles and miles, they ran – the stag in front, the king and his dogs behind.

Then suddenly, the stag leapt high into the air over a ravine. The dogs were going so fast that they fell, helter skelter, down the cliff. The king's horse, too, was running at breakneck speed and out of control. In any moment, horse and rider would be falling to their death. Quickly, Edmund said what he thought would be his last prayer.

"I thank you, Lord, for all you have given me. I am sorry for the wrong I have done – especially to Dunstan. If I live, I will make it right."

At that, somehow or other, the horse stopped. Edmund found himself, sitting in the saddle and peering down into the deep gorge.

When he returned home, he immediately went to find Dunstan. He made the monk take a horse and they rode together to Glastonbury. There, the king proclaimed Dunstan the new abbot, and promised to help the abbey in every way he could.

This was Dunstan's opportunity. As a young man, he had thought how different the abbey was from the great days of the past. Now, he could begin changing it back to its old glory. Slowly and carefully, Dunstan set about his work. His monks had to meet in the church to pray together several times a day. They could not own anything, and they had to work for the abbey.

At this time, it was not only England that needed change. The vikings had fought and raided all over Europe. Everywhere it was the abbeys that they had attacked and burnt, and everywhere the abbeys were in ruins, their monks in despair. But now people were trying to improve things. They were trying to repair buildings, and make the abbeys holy places once again.

For sixteen years, Dunstan worked at Glastonbury. Then a new king came to the throne, a king who did not like Dunstan, and he had to go abroad. In some ways, this was lucky. In Europe he could see the changes other people were making. And when he came back after seven years abroad, he could copy some foreign ideas.

But there was also a different kind of life ahead of him. Another new king made Dunstan Archbishop of Canterbury, the head of the Church in England. For years, he was very busy. He worked for the whole country in the way that before he had worked for his abbey. He created laws and built churches, always aiming to bring greatness once again to English Christianity.

It was a life full of work and worry. But Dunstan still spent a lot of time in prayer. At night, he would go into Canterbury Cathedral, or into the church of the abbey next to it. There he would pray. One night, as he was praying in this way, he thought he heard the song of all the saints around him. The music was so beautiful that he wept to hear it.

By the end of his life, Dunstan had made great changes in the Church in England. Many abbeys and churches were once again holy places. Of course, he did not make the changes alone. A lot of people helped the work in different ways. Together, they proved that glories do not have to be past glories. With faith, it is possible to make things now as marvellous as they have ever been.

Dunstan died in the year 988. His feast is on 19th May.

Anselm

The sound of a nearby stream could be heard in the abbey. It was a soft spring day in France, and the monks were happy in their work. One of the youngest, Osbern, was showing a visitor round the buildings.

"He gave up everything," Osbern was explaining enthusiastically. "He gave up his family, his hopes, his home, his country. Then he set off from Italy across the mountains. The journey was so hard that he had to suck melted snow for drink. And even when he arrived in France his travelling was not over. He went from monastery to monastery and from school to school. But at last, he came here to Bec, and here he stayed. You have seen his cell – how bare it is."

The visitor smiled and nodded.

"And I already know what happened here," he said. "Your Anselm grew into such a famous teacher that students now come to him from all over Europe." He paused before adding quietly. "He must have a strong arm."

"A strong arm?" Osbern asked.

"To beat knowledge into the thick skins of boys like you."

"No," replied Osbern. "You don't understand. He does not flog us along the road to wisdom. I once heard him say that children who were beaten would grow into stupid brutes. We should think of the goldsmith, he said. The goldsmith makes beautiful things by gently pressing and tapping his gold – always by being gentle. Parents and teachers must do the same, only even more gently."

The visitor looked a little puzzled. In those days, every teacher used canes and blows to enforce his lessons. How could this one be different? Perhaps his lessons were too easy.

"What does he teach?" the visitor asked at last.

"The same things as other teachers," answered Osbern.

He was quiet for a moment thinking about his answer.

"But also something else," he went on. "He teaches that you must look at yourself. Not at how you are outside, but into yourself, deep into yourself. To see what kind of a person you are. That makes you understand that you're bad and selfish." He shuddered. "Very bad. And it makes you hate being like that. So you stop boasting and thinking you are important. Instead, you know you are not worth much."

He paused.

"But then, you wonder how God must see you. What God must think of your selfishness. And that's a frightening thought. So, you try to do nothing that God does not want, to give up everything except God's will." He paused a second time. "Then at last you can be happy and free. This is what he teaches."

"Everything except God's will?"

"He says everything should be as God wants. It is better for the whole world to disappear than for someone even to blink in a way God does not want."

Again the visitor was silent, thinking about what he had heard.

"A hard lesson to teach without blows," he said.

"But he does it," Osbern insisted. "He uses gentleness. Listen – when I first came here, I didn't want to learn anything. All I wanted to do was to play, and to have fun. I expected to be beaten for that. But he didn't beat me, and he didn't speak roughly to me. He was always gentle and kind. So that in the end I began to love him. And slowly, bit by bit, he taught me to look at myself and to understand. He demanded more and more of me. And now I don't mind doing anything he asks."

They had reached the schoolroom, a small stone building with a thatched roof. The visitor glanced inside. A few students were sitting on benches with writing slates on their knees. In front of them was their teacher. His voice rose and fell gently, and the expression on his face was calm. The boys on the benches sat and listened, their eyes fixed on him.

The visitor turned to Osbern.

"Your Anselm is a remarkable man," he said.

At that time, Anselm was Abbot of Bec in France. He was known far and wide for his teaching, his writing and his love of God. Since he behaved with everyone as he did with his pupils, his mildness was also famous. It had the strange effect of making even violent men grow quiet with him.

The ruler of Anselm's part of France was Duke William. The duke earned himself the name of Conqueror when he became king of England. He sailed there with ships and soldiers, and battled his way to the throne. That was his character. He was a man who would allow nothing and no one to stand in his way. But in Anselm's presence William was calm, and when he died, he asked for the abbot to come to him.

But even Anselm could not tame everyone. With such people, he proved that his gentleness was not weakness. Nothing they threatened or did could move him from the will of God.

After William's death, his son, Rufus, became king of England. He was a fierce man, more violent than his father had been.

"Like an untamed bull," Anselm once said.

As king, Rufus did nothing to help the Church,

The boys on the benches sat and listened, their eyes fixed on him.

and when the Archbishop of Canterbury died, he refused to allow a new one. Instead, he took the money from the cathedral's lands for himself.

After three years of this, Rufus fell ill. His sickness grew so bad that everyone thought he would die. Lying close to death, this fierce man suddenly became frightened of God's judgement. He had done so much against God in his life – what would God do to him now?

One thing at least he could put right. At last, he decided to make a new archbishop. But who should it be? The bishops agreed that Anselm, who was in England just then, would be the best choice.

Anselm did not want to be archbishop. When the bishops told him that he was their choice, he asked them to find someone else. They insisted, so he knelt at their feet and wept, begging them to show mercy.

It is the custom that a new archbishop must take hold of a special staff. The bishops brought the staff to Anselm. He refused to touch it and clenched his fingers into fists. The bishops seized his hands, unwound the fingers, and put them on the staff. Then, they dragged him to the king.

Finally, when he saw it was God's will, Anselm agreed. Now, he was head of the Church in England, and responsible for the good of English Christianity. Like Dunstan over 100 years ago, he wanted to use his position to do good.

But Anselm soon learnt that the king was

against him. Rufus had not died during his illness. When he recovered, he forgot his terror of God, and went back to his old ways.

At that time, although England was a Christian country, many people did not lead Christian lives. Anselm thought the king should help change this.

"What help do you want?" Rufus asked.

"Years ago, the bishops used to meet in councils," Anselm answered evenly. "They would discuss what was wrong, and think of ways to make things better. You could, if you wished, command us to hold a council now."

"I will do that, when I decide," the king replied, his anger rising. "And not when you suggest it. Another time! And anyway, what would you talk about at your council?"

"We would talk about the evil in the country."

"And what good would that do you?"

When Anselm answered his voice was still quiet and gentle.

"It would do no good to me," he said. "But it would do good to God and perhaps to you."

"Enough," barked the king. "No more about it!"

Seeing that the king was not going to agree, Anselm changed the subject.

"There is another kind of help I wanted to ask," he said. "Many abbeys in England do not have abbots. Their monks are not living good lives. Please make abbots for these abbeys so they can become holy places once again."

This was too much for the king.

"Is that any of your business?" he bellowed. "The abbeys are mine, and I'll do what I want with them."

"They are yours to guard and defend," Anselm replied without anger, "but they are not yours to attack and rob."

Rufus stared hard into the eyes of his archbishop.

"You can be quite sure," he said slowly, spitting out each word, "that I hate everything you say. And I will do nothing for you."

The council and the abbeys were not Anselm's only problems with Rufus. It was the custom in those days for a new archbishop to go to Rome, in order to receive the pope's blessing. But Rufus would not let Anselm go. He said that if the archbishop swore to be loyal to the pope, he could not be loyal to his king as well. It was like stealing the crown, he said.

There was no changing the king's mind. Even Anselm could not tame this wild bull. What was worse, with Rufus in power, he could not do his duty as archbishop. But Anselm would not give in, and act against God. At last, he decided that the only way to protest was to go abroad to France. This was his first exile.

When Rufus died, a new king took the English throne, and Anselm returned. Again, he was not able to work, and again he had to go away. At last, after this second exile, he made an agreement with the king, and came back to England for good.

Now he could begin the work he wanted to do. He called the great meeting of the bishops which he had planned so long ago. At the council, they decided on ways to help Christianity in England. And so, after many years of waiting, Anselm's gentle firmness won out in the end.

He continued to work for the Church for the rest of his life. Always he was the same person who had been a loved teacher and abbot. Though he was kind with everyone, nothing could shift him from the will of God.

Anselm died in 1109, and his feast is on 21st April.

Thomas Becket

"Do I look like a saint?" Thomas asked, laughing.

King Henry regarded him up and down. Thomas, the chancellor, was holding his arms out to display the bright silks of his sleeves. Rings glittered on his fingers, and a gold clasp shone beneath the fur collar of his cloak. Everything about him was splendid and expensive.

"Well..." answered the king. He shook his head slightly, in agreement that this was not exactly the way that saints looked.

"And have I lived like a saint?"

Again the king shook his head a little.

"A life of pleasure," Thomas went on. "A life of feasts and banquets – the finest food and wines. A life of buying things – gold and silver and jewels. I've even been in your wars, rode in battle and fought. Is this the kind of man to be archbishop?"

The king smiled.

"You will not change my mind, Thomas," he said. "I want you to be my Archbishop of Canterbury. I have decided – you are to be head of the Church in England."

"And if the bishops do not agree?" Thomas

asked. "If they say they want a holy man for archbishop, and not a pleasure-lover?"

Henry snorted, and waved his hand.

"I am king. The bishops will do as I say. And you, Thomas, will also do as I say. You are to be archbishop."

The chancellor was quiet for a moment, thinking about the king's command. As he thought, his face became slowly more serious.

"It will be the end of our friendship," he said at last. "You will expect me to be loyal to you. But if I am archbishop, I will be loyal to the Church. We shall fight. There will be constant fighting between us."

"We shall see," answered Henry. "We shall see."

So, Thomas Becket became Archbishop of Canterbury, and a new life began for him. Before, he had always dressed in the finest clothes. Now he wore the plain habit of the monk. And beneath the habit was a rough shirt that rubbed painfully against his skin.

Before, he had been friends with all the important people of England. He had been happy talking and joking with them. Now he took poor pilgrims into his room, fed them and washed their feet.

Before, he had loved to eat rich food and drink fine wine at feasts and banquets. Now, he provided food and wine for his guests, while he himself fed on bread and water.

But there was also another way in which Thomas's life was changed. He had for years been the servant and friend of the king. They had worked together and enjoyed each other's company. But when Thomas became archbishop, the friendship began to die.

It was only little things at first. Thomas wanted to give a parish to one of his priests. The lord of the area wanted someone else to have the job, and the king took the lord's side. When that was settled, there was an argument about a tax on land which Henry planned to set. Thomas argued that priests should not have to pay the tax. The king said they must.

There could be no end to these disputes. Henry wanted more power over the Church, and Thomas was determined not to give it. In this way, the two men were set against each other.

Gradually, things got worse and worse. Henry, who had once loved Thomas, began to feel annoyed with him. His annoyance turned to dislike, and his dislike turned to hate. He became determined not only to get the power he wanted but also to destroy his old friend.

At Henry's command, a document was prepared. The document said many things, but the main point was simple. The king should be more important than the pope to English priests. They should be loyal to the king first and the pope only second.

Thomas, along with the other bishops, was asked to sign the document. He refused, and Henry's hatred increased. There must, he thought, be some way to use the law against this archbishop. But since Thomas had done nothing wrong, the law had to be twisted to harm him.

Thomas was called to court about the case of one of Henry's knights. The case was nothing, and anyway, the court had no power over the archbishop. He refused to go. The refusal, said Henry, was treason, and Thomas must travel to Northampton to explain himself.

By now, everyone knew that Thomas was hated by the king. One by one, his friends stopped visiting him. Even the bishops did not stand by him, and when he arrived at Northampton, he found himself alone except for a few faithful priests.

A great council was held to discuss the traitor. Thomas had to wait in a room outside. The council would not allow him to appear before them and defend himself. Even in the outside room no one was permitted to speak to him. Finally, at the end of the day, the Earl of Leicester, one of the council, came with news.

"I have to announce," he said, "that your sentence…"

"Sentence?" asked Thomas angrily. "I have not had a trial. How can there be a sentence?"

"Even so, my lord," the earl went on. "Your sentence…"

"Stop," commanded Thomas. "As your archbishop, I forbid you to say anything more."

The order surprised the earl. Not knowing what to do, he left to ask advice. When he had gone, Thomas strode out with his priests behind him.

They had to pass through a large hall in order to get outside. It was full of nobles loyal to the king, and they jeered as Thomas passed among them.

"Traitor!" one shouted in his ear.

Thomas stumbled over something on the floor and nearly fell. The nobles round him pointed and laughed. But at last, he and his priests were at the door. They collected their horses and rode away.

In the streets everything was different. The ordinary people had little love for the king, and knew of the plots against the archbishop. They lined the way to watch him pass, kneeling as he rode by to ask his blessing.

That night Thomas left Northampton in disguise. Perhaps he was frightened. Perhaps he remembered the example of Anselm seventy years earlier. Faced with a cruel king, Anselm had gone in protest to France. Whatever the reason, Thomas decided that he too must leave his country.

He spent more than six years abroad. They were busy years, for he had to work hard with the pope and with foreign kings, trying to make Henry give in. But these years were also busy in a different way. Thomas spent a lot of time during his exile thinking, praying and growing closer to God.

At last, a peace was made with the king, and the archbishop could return to Canterbury. It was a triumphant return. There were people cheering all along the road from the coast to the city. At every village he passed, the church choir would appear and sing songs of thanks and rejoicing.

But Henry still hated Thomas, and was still determined to ruin him. In England, it is the Archbishop of Canterbury who crowns kings. Henry wanted his son crowned, and he ordered other bishops to do it. In fear, the bishops obeyed.

By doing this, they were acting against their archbishop and their Church, and they left Thomas little choice. He declared them cut off from the Church.

Henry was furious. To him, Thomas's action seemed like treason.

It was Christmas and he was in France with his nobles.

"I curse all of you," he shouted. "All of you whom I have helped and who will not help me. Look at the gifts you have had from me! And one priest – one priest – is too much for you!"

The nobles tried to calm him, but he was not to be calmed.

"Will no one rid me of this turbulent priest?" he cried.

That same evening, four of his knights left France and set off on their journey to Canterbury.

They arrived in the late afternoon just before the end of the year. When they asked to see the archbishop, they were shown in to him.

"The king orders you," said one of them, "to forgive the bishops, and to allow them back into the Church."

"Of course, I am ready to do that," Thomas answered. "But first they must accept the Church's authority over them."

The answer infuriated the knights.

"Leave the country," they said. "You will have no peace until you do."

"It is no good threatening me," he replied. "I will not leave. I ran away once because I was frightened. But I have come back, and I know now that it is my duty to stay – whatever might happen."

Some of Thomas's servants were in the room, watching everything. One of the knights turned to them.

"Guard him," he ordered.

"That's easily done," Thomas said. "I will not go away."

At this the knights went outside and began to put on their armour. Thomas's priests and servants urged him to take refuge in the cathedral, but he refused. Then, through the dusk came the chanting of evening prayers.

"Vespers," said one of the priests. "It is your duty to be in the cathedral."

Thomas could not deny this, and without hurry, he set off in procession.

It was dark in the cathedral except for the weak light of the candles. Though the priests with Thomas wanted to bar the door, he would not let them.

"We must not turn God's house into a fortress," he said.

He had not reached the altar before strange noises interrupted the prayers and the chants. The sound of clanking armour could be heard among the ancient stones of the cathedral. And rough voices were shouting about kings and traitors and archbishops.

Many of the priests and monks in the procession fled and hid. A few remained with Thomas. The little group of unarmed men stood waiting by a column.

"Where is the traitor archbishop?" an angry voice called somewhere in the dim church.

"I am here," answered Thomas, "and no traitor but a priest."

"Over there," the voice shouted to his companions. The clanking of metal could be heard ever louder, then out of the gloom appeared the first of the knights. His sword was in his hand, he was covered in armour from head to toe and the helmet's visor was down. Behind him were the other three.

And gathering behind them was a frightened

group of Canterbury citizens. One of the knights turned towards the people, and with his sword pointed at them, kept them back.

The others ran to the archbishop. They seized hold of him to drag him from the church. Even these men did not want to spill blood in such a

holy place. But Thomas would not budge. There was a struggle and he pushed one of them away.

The knight staggered back, almost fell, then caught his balance. He lifted his sword, and with a roar, rushed at the archbishop. One of the priests put out his arm to protect his master. The sword cut him to the bone, and grazed Thomas's head.

Now the other knights joined in. One brought his sword crashing down on the archbishop – again on his head. Then, back up, and a third blow to the head.

Thomas fell to his knees.

"For Jesus and the Church," he said quietly, "I am ready to die."

The third knight swung his sword – at the head again – and Thomas fell down dead.

"Let's go," the knight shouted. "He'll never move again."

They ran from the cathedral, their armour clanking as they went.

"The king's men," they bawled. "The king's men."

Behind them on the floor of the cathedral lay the body of someone who had also once been a king's man. But in time, he had become God's man instead. And to his praise, he had remained God's man right until death.

Thomas Becket died in 1170 on 29th December – the date we celebrate his feast.

Thomas More

Two or three of the chancellor's family had gathered by the window to watch. The king's barge could be seen waiting on the river, and there in the garden was the king himself. It was a great favour to have him visit in this way. He had come to dinner more like a friend than a king, and now like a friend, he was taking the air with his arm round the chancellor.

It was 350 years after the death of Thomas Becket. The king was now a different Henry – Henry VIII. And his chancellor was a different Thomas – Thomas More. But in some ways, the stories of these different kings and their different chancellors are very similar.

There was the sound of laughter from the garden, the loud laughter of the king. No doubt it was at some joke that Thomas had made. Respectful servants stood by the riverbank, and from the house the family watched. At last the king left, with a great show of thanks and affection.

When Thomas returned to the house, he was met by Margaret, one of his daughters, and her husband William. They wanted to know what the king had said and how he had behaved.

"You are a lucky man, father," William said when Thomas had finished. "I have never seen the king so friendly with anyone – to talk like that and to walk arm in arm!"

"His majesty has been very good to me," Thomas replied. "I can think of no one in the country he has treated more kindly. But even so, I have no reason to be proud of his friendship."

He fell silent.

"Why do you say that?" William asked, puzzled.

"You know that our armies are fighting in France," he answered. "Well, my head cannot win the king a single castle there. But if it could, my head would certainly go."

It was not, though, for a castle in France that Thomas eventually lost his head. It was for his loyalty to the Church.

Henry had no son. Every time his wife, Catherine, gave birth to one, the baby died. In those days, the king needed a son to inherit the throne after him, and Henry became desperate for a little boy. He must find another wife, he thought. Perhaps someone different could bear him a son.

But Christian marriage is forever, and the Church does not allow divorce. So, Henry began to wonder if perhaps his marriage to Catherine was not a proper marriage. Perhaps he had never really been married at all. If that was so, why not marry someone else now?

The only problem was the Church. Henry needed the Church to say he was not married, and to agree to marry him. The pope said the Church would study the matter. But that was not enough for Henry. He wanted to marry right away. He had chosen his new woman, Anne Boleyn, and he wanted to make her his wife and queen.

The pope was a long way off in Rome. Henry had all the power in England and would not wait for an answer. He ordered the archbishop to marry him and to crown Anne. When the pope's answer did come, it said that Henry's marriage to Catherine was a proper marriage after all.

Thomas watched all this happening. He saw Henry disobeying the pope and he feared that even worse would come. For nearly a thousand years, the English Church had been part of the Catholic Church. Now, the king seemed to be trying to take over the Church for himself.

Thomas thought he had little choice. He gave up being chancellor. From now on, he would live a quiet life, following his religion and disturbing nobody.

But Henry was a bully. He could not be happy if people quietly disagreed with him. He wanted everyone to give in and say he was right. Anyone who would not surrender must be threatened and hurt, perhaps destroyed.

About that time, a mad woman became famous by making speeches against the king. At first people did not realise that she was mad. Some listened to her, and did not report what she said. This was a kind of treason and investigations were started. Although Thomas had never spoken to the woman alone, the king ordered that he too should be investigated.

He was called before a committee to explain himself. Before leaving for the meeting he did what he always did at such times. He went to confession and received communion.

Then, he set off down the river with his son-in-law. William was very worried. If Thomas was proved to be a traitor the whole family would be ruined.

There were four men on the committee. They sat in a huge room behind a long table, with Thomas standing alone before them.

"Please sit," one of them said. It was the new chancellor, who had taken Thomas's old job.

"I should prefer to stand," Thomas answered.

"As you wish," said the chancellor. He coughed. "His majesty has done a lot for you. He has given you work and gifts. He has helped you in every way."

"That is certainly true," Thomas agreed.

The chancellor waited a moment before going on.

"The king dearly wants to help you now. He

*They sat in a huge room behind a long table, with
Thomas standing alone before them.*

will give you a job again, and his friendship, if…"

There was a silence.

"If…?" prompted Thomas.

"If you will agree that the marriage to Catherine was not a marriage. And that Anne is his wife and our queen."

"I have nothing more to say about that," Thomas replied.

"Nothing?"

"Nothing."

When the chancellor saw that Thomas would not change his mind, he became angry.

"There are other things to consider," he said coldly. "The mad woman of Kent, for example. You knew her, so you can be tried for treason. The penalty, as you know, is death. And a traitor can leave nothing to his family. They will be beggars."

"My lords," said Thomas. "These terrors are arguments for children and not for me."

On the way back, William was eager to find out what had happened. But since his father-in-law was quiet, he did not like to speak. At last, Thomas began to laugh quietly to himself.

"I am glad to see you are happy," William said.

"Yes," Thomas admitted.

"Have they decided you are not a traitor, then?"

Thomas looked puzzled for a moment.

"The truth is," he said, "that I'd forgotten all

about that. Do you want to know why I was so happy?"

William nodded.

"It was because I was thinking that I'd managed to trip Satan up. I said so much in front of the committee that now I will never be able to turn back. I will have to stick to the truth."

A few days later, one of the committee came to tell Thomas, that he would not be charged. The man was an old friend of Thomas's and unhappy about his trouble.

"This is a dangerous game you're playing," he warned. "You must have more sense. Do what the king says. You know the saying – a king's anger means death."

"Is that all?" asked Thomas. "Then, there's not much difference between us, is there? Only this, that I'll die today, and you'll die tomorrow."

The friend's warning soon proved true. Henry seemed determined to destroy his old chancellor. He ordered parliament to make a new law. Everyone had to swear an oath saying that the pope was wrong, and that Catherine had never been Henry's wife. But there was worse than that. Part of the oath also said that Henry, and not the pope, was the head of the Church in England. Thomas's worst fears had come true. Henry was cutting England off from the Catholic Church, and from the other Christians of the world.

To refuse the oath was treason, but Thomas, of course, refused. He was arrested and locked away in the Tower of London. When his daughter Margaret visited him there, she could not help showing her sorrow at the cold, bare cell.

"Don't be sad," Thomas said. "I promise you that I would have lived like this long ago if it had not been for the family."

There was a noise from the courtyard below, and Thomas and Margaret went to the window. Some monks who had also refused the oath were being prepared for execution. Guards were strapping them to wooden frames, ready to have them dragged by horses through the streets outside.

"Look," said Thomas to his daughter. "Do you notice how happy those holy fathers are – almost like bridegrooms going to their wedding? What a difference there is between them and me! Because they have lived religious lives, God has allowed them to go to him straight away. But I have had an easy life, always with the best of everything, so he is making me wait."

Eventually, Thomas was taken to trial and found guilty. The judges asked him if he had anything else to say in his defence.

"Only this," he answered. "Stephen was killed hundreds of years ago for believing in Christ, and Paul was there at the death. He was not one of the killers, but he looked after their coats as they stoned Stephen. But Paul became a Christian, and now he and Stephen are happy together in heaven. Today, my lords, you are sending me to my death. But I pray that we will meet in heaven, and like Paul and Stephen, we will be happy there together."

For a week after that, Thomas was kept in his cell. He was weak by now, and when he was finally taken to the scaffold, he had to ask to be helped up the ladder. Even then, his humour did not leave him.

"Please give me a hand up," he joked. "As for my getting back down again – I'll see to that myself."

On the scaffold, he knelt and said his prayers, then stood and turned to the executioner.

"Don't be unhappy, man," he said cheerfully. "But I warn you, I have a short neck. So, take good aim and make sure you don't miss."

He laid his head on the block, then lifted it, and moved his beard out of the way.

"At least my beard," he said, "has never committed treason."

Then, he prayed again, and the axe came down.

Thomas More died in 1535. His feast is on 22nd June.

Edmund Campion

The servant could not understand it. Not that the task itself was difficult. He must stay there by the front door and answer to everyone who knocked. Certain people must be let in and sent up to the chapel at the back of the house. Certain other people must be turned away. And if anyone suspicious came, he must warn the master. There was nothing difficult in that.

It was even easy enough to see why he had been given the job – just as he had often been given the same job before. His fellow servants wanted to be up there, at the back of the house, in the chapel.

But what he could not understand was what it was all for. Why did his master and mistress take such risks and lose so much money? He had watched their wealth going down over the last twenty years as they paid their extra fines and taxes. And he knew of friends and cousins of theirs who had been sent to prison or abroad – one even who had been executed.

Of course, he would not betray them and put them in danger. He had worked for the family all his life, and he was loyal to them. But being loyal did not help him understand the risks they took.

And for so little! If it was Christianity they wanted, there was safe Christianity enough in the village. No one denied that the parson there was a good man. And his church gave prayers and services. The parson even said that his services were the best kind. He said that the old way in the village, the old Mass that had been said in England for centuries, was unchristian and wrong. Men at the universities had written books to prove it. And Queen Elizabeth herself agreed.

There was a knock at the door, which the servant answered. In the dim light of the early morning, he recognised two neighbours, the last of the guests. Their horses had already been taken away, and they stood outside the door with the same air of quiet excitement as the other guests.

They hurried past him and up the stairs, and he shook his head in silent disbelief. It was a gesture he had been making all morning. These people were risking everything in order to take part in something he did not understand.

"It is a miracle," his master had explained once to him. "Bread which has been made by human beings becomes the body of Jesus Christ. We are allowed to be joined to him by eating the bread."

"And in the village church?" the servant had asked. "At communion?"

"Nothing happens," his master had answered. "The parson does not even claim to be able to change the bread he blesses. It's bread, just bread.

And that place you call a church is only a building of stone and wood. But for us, our Church is our people, alive with the spirit of God. And with our priest, the bread becomes the body of Jesus. We can share in that."

"Too hard for me," the servant muttered to himself remembering the words.

He sat on a bench by the door and waited. The world outside the door was still asleep, and in the distance he heard a single cock crow. Somewhere, at the back of the house, something was happening which he could not understand.

For nearly an hour, he sat there, and then he heard voices from inside the house. The guests were coming downstairs. He stood up and moved respectfully to one side of the door. Most would leave fairly quickly, he knew. It would be dangerous for them to stay too long at the house.

He opened the door, watched them step outside into the yard, breathe deeply in the early morning air and wait for their horses to be brought. Soon the yard was full of the bustle of leaving – horses, stablehands and farewells.

The servant turned back inside. Standing there were his master and the tall priest, dressed now like all the other guests.

"This is Michael, Father," the master said. "He has kept watch for us."

"He belongs to the Church?" the priest asked.

Kneeling and bowing his neck, the servant felt a touch on his head, and heard the words of a Latin prayer.

"No, Father, but perhaps he would accept the blessing of a Catholic priest."

The servant looked into the face of the priest, and something about the man made him agree. He nodded.

"You will have to kneel, Michael," his master explained.

Kneeling and bowing his neck, the servant felt a touch on his head, and heard the words of a Latin prayer. He waited, uncertain what to do next, until he felt the hand of the priest under his arm, gently lifting him up.

That priest was Edmund Campion.

He had been born a few years after the death of Thomas More, and had grown up in a country torn apart by religious differences. When Elizabeth became queen, she made England Protestant by law. At first, the Catholics were left almost in peace. But the queen and her government were afraid they might try to take over, and gradually the laws against them increased.

At that time Edmund worked at Oxford University, and he had to belong to the Church of England to keep his job. Eventually, however, after much thought, he made the main decision of his life. He gave everything up, and left England to become a Catholic abroad.

For some years, he led a quiet life as a professor in Prague, training to become a Jesuit priest. But then he was sent home by his superiors, as one of the early missionaries to Protestant England. He had to travel in disguise, and he knew that if he was caught, he would be tortured and probably executed.

His mission lasted only one year. For that year, he travelled up and down the country, celebrating Mass and hearing confessions. He also wrote two books saying that Catholicism was true Christianity, and that English Catholics did not want to overthrow the queen. The books were banned and burnt, but still people got copies of them and read them. His writings made him famous, and the government was determined to catch him.

The chance came when he visited a well-known Catholic house in Berkshire. A government spy, George Eliot, happened to visit when Edmund was preaching. He left to warn the local judges, and came back with armed men to arrest the priest. By this time Edmund was hiding in the house, but after a long search he was found.

He was taken to the Tower of London, kept in filthy cells and tortured on the rack. Ropes were tied to his wrists and ankles and his body was stretched until he was in agony. The torturers wanted to get information from him about the Catholics he had visited, and about plots against the queen. He told them nothing.

After several weeks, he was brought out of his

cell to take part in what was called a conference. He had become so famous that the government wanted to prove his ideas wrong. So, they took him to hear the arguments of men from the Protestant Church of England. The government hoped that these men would beat Edmund in the discussion.

Their task should have been easy. They had books and secretaries to help them argue, while Edmund had nothing. He was not even allowed to give his side, only to comment on theirs. But still he insisted on the truth.

"Put it in writing," one of his opponents challenged him at one stage.

"Give me pen and ink," he answered, "and I will."

"I cannot give you pen and ink."

"I mean get me permission to write."

"I don't know why you do not have permission. So, I won't get it for you."

"Ask the the queen if I might have freedom to put my case. I have listened to yours. It is only fair that I should put mine."

"I will ask nothing for you."

And so the discussion went on.

There were four of these conferences. When they were finally over, Edmund was taken back to the torture chamber and racked again – this time so fiercely that he thought his torturers meant to kill him.

Finally, he had to go to trial, along with fourteen other priests. Since the government did not want to appear unfair, they did not charge the men with being Catholics or priests. Instead, they said they had plotted to kill the queen. It was not true, but that made no difference at this trial. As everyone expected, the verdict was guilty.

After the verdict had been given, Edmund was allowed to speak. He insisted that he and his companions had been tried for their religion and not for treason.

"In condemning us," he added, "you condemn all your own ancestors, all that was once the glory of England, the island of saints. For what have we taught that they did not teach?"

Then, the sentence was passed. Edmund and his companions were to be hung, drawn and quartered. The remains of their bodies would be displayed around London to discourage others from following the same path.

Before the day of execution arrived, Edmund had a visitor in his cell. It was George Eliot, the spy who had betrayed him. Ever since the arrest Eliot had gone in fear for his life, thinking that the Catholics would want to take revenge on him.

Edmund offered the man both his forgiveness and the chance of safety – a job with a German duke he knew. Eliot refused. But the goaler who watched the meeting was so affected by Edmund's kindness that he began to think more about his religion. Eventually, he became a Catholic.

On the day of execution, Edmund and two others were strapped onto wooden frames. Horses dragged them through the streets to Tyburn, the public place of execution just outside London. A crowd lined the way, and even more people were waiting there for them. Some came to mock, others to stare, and others still to admire.

Edmund was put on a cart with the rope round his neck. It was the custom that a condemned man could speak to the crowd before he died. He insisted once more that he was to die not for any plot against the government but for his religion. Then, after Edmund's prayer, the guards pulled the cart away, and the dreadful punishment began.

Edmund Campion died on 1st December 1581. He was declared a saint in 1970. His feast is 25th October.

Anne Line

The priest stood in the doorway of the house and took deep breaths. His heart was still racing, his lungs ached and he had a stitch in his side. Putting his hands on his stomach, he bent double and waited a moment or two.

It was only when he straightened himself that he looked about him. He was in a small courtyard, and though it was the middle of the day, the yard was made dusky by the overhanging houses round it. The only way out was the narrow alley he had entered by.

He breathed deeply and thought hard. Why had he not been more careful? It was dangerous in England for Catholic priests – he knew that. You had to wear a disguise and pretend you were an ordinary gentleman. And you had to avoid acting like a Catholic. He had been told often enough what to do – and what not to do.

He must not call another priest "Father". He must not speak too much of the saints. And when he crossed London Bridge he must be especially careful. Above him on the gate would be the heads of Catholic martyrs. But he must show no respect for them.

The only way out was the narrow alley he had entered by.

All these things he had remembered. And still, he had given himself away only a few days after landing in England. At an inn! It was at the inns you had to be most careful – everyone said so. But then, his mistake was such a little one.

It had been dinner time, with several guests round the inn table. By chance, one of them had asked the priest to say grace. He had bowed his head to offer thanks, and without thinking had made the sign of the cross at the end of the prayer.

Immediately, he knew that the other guests were looking at him. Do not cross yourself in England, he had been warned. Or they will guess you are a Catholic. But it was impossible to remember everything. And now he had given himself away.

It was not that he was very afraid of being caught, or even of dying. Every priest who came to England knew he might be executed. But he had come to the country to work, and to help those who needed him. And so far he had done nothing except travel from the coast to London.

After his mistake, the other guests had looked at him in silence. Then, they started on their meal. But half way through, a little man sitting at the end of the table made an excuse and left. Could he be a spy? Fearing this, the priest got up from the table himself.

His first thought was to get his horse from the stables, but the little man was in the yard talking to two others. They saw the priest and called to him. Pretending not to hear, he turned and hurried into the street, trying not to run. Were they after him? He went first into one street, then another, and finally into the narrow alley that led to this courtyard.

But the question was what to do now. He held his stomach and breathed more steadily.

"Who are you?" a rough voice called. A man was advancing towards him across the courtyard. "What do you want? You do not live here. What's your business?"

"I am looking for a friend," the priest answered.

"Oh? Who?"

"I'm sorry, it is the wrong place," the priest said, and pushed past the man, back through the alley and into the street.

What should he do? He could not return to the inn, and it would be dangerous to arrive at a different inn with no horse. He must find Mistress Line's house. He would be safe there.

The priest had had heard much of Mistress Line abroad, and had even met her husband once years ago. The man had suffered a lot for being a Catholic. His family had taken away his money, and he had been sent to prison for attending Mass. So, in the end, he had gone to live abroad, where he could follow his own religion. Now he was dead, and his widow, Anne, was risking her life to protect priests.

The priest knew she had been a Protestant once.

But a few years ago, still a teenager, she had become Catholic. Her family was furious. Although her father was a rich man, he had refused to give her any money to get married. So, instead of getting a rich Protestant husband, she had married a poor Catholic.

The priest must find her now. But how? It was years since he had been in England, and he had never known London well.

He looked down the street. There was some sort of commotion at the other end of it, a large gang of men making a lot of noise. And there among them, the little guest from the inn!

The priest turned and walked quickly in the other direction. He followed one alley and then another, before coming out into a large street lined with shops.

"What road is this?" he asked a man who was passing with a barrow of vegetables.

"Cheapside, master," the man replied. "Are you a stranger here?"

"From the north," the priest said, and walked quickly away. Was it even dangerous to be a stranger these days?

But if this was Cheapside he could find his way. He walked quickly past two entrances, then turned left into a third. Not much further now. Somewhere in the streets behind him was the gang of searchers – he must hurry.

He turned again. There was the garden door in

the wall just as he had been told. He pushed open the door, closed it, and hurried up to the main door of the house.

He knocked and waited, knocked again. Finally, a servant opened the door. Behind him in the corridor was a woman of less than thirty years.

"Mistress Line?" the priest asked.

"Yes?"

"I am a priest," he said. "I have letters. I knew your husband."

"Come, Father," she answered, lifting a hand towards him in welcome.

He stepped inside and closed the door behind him. At last, he was safe.

For three years Anne Line dedicated herself to this kind of work. At that time it was against the law to be a Catholic priest in England or to help one. The sentence for these offences was death. But despite this, priests continued to arrive in the country, and men and women like Anne continued to shelter them.

For those three years, she lived in a large house in London. Most of the priests who arrived in the country were sent to her. They were Englishmen, trained abroad, and she would take them in, care for them, hide them and arrange meetings with other priests. Eventually, they would go to the Catholics in different parts of the country.

After three years of the work, Anne was known

to a lot of people and her house was no longer safe. She moved from it and took rooms elsewhere. Although the new priests did not come to her now, she still arranged illegal Masses, and it was one of these that led to her arrest.

At the beginning of February, a large number of people gathered at her rooms for Mass. A little altar was ready in a back room, with a chalice, a cloth and candles. The visiting priest put on his vestments and prepared himself to say Mass.

But some neighbours noticed how many people were going to Mistress Anne's. They became suspicious and informed the authorities. It was not long before men were hammering at the door and trampling through the rooms. Their entry was so sudden that there was no time to hide the altar or the priest. There was only time for him to take off his vestments.

The searchers burst into the room and began their questions. What were all these people doing there? Was it a Mass? Did they not know Mass was illegal? Where was the priest? Why did no one answer?

Since the altar was still there, it was useless to pretend they had not come for a Mass. But no one would admit that the priest had arrived, and no one would say who he was.

Among the shouting and confusion, the priest noticed that a door had been left open and unguarded. He moved quietly towards it. None of the searchers noticed his movements. Suddenly, he was away, slamming the door behind him. In a moment, he was up the stairs and inside the hiding place which Anne had prepared for him.

The searchers looked everywhere, but they found nothing. The priest had escaped, so all they could do was make a few arrests, and release the other guests on bail. Anne was among those arrested.

She was taken to prison and kept there for just over three weeks. Her health had been bad for years and she was afraid that the cold and damp of the prison would kill her before she could go for trial. She wanted to be tried so that people would know what her crime was. Somehow she managed to survive long enough, and at the end of February, she was carried before her judges in a chair.

The charge against her was that she had sheltered priests.

"Is it true?" the judges asked.

She refused to answer yes or no.

"My lords," she replied instead, "I am only sad that I could not help a thousand more."

There was little evidence against her – only the altar in her house and her defiance. But for the judges, those were enough. She was found guilty, and sentenced to death.

On the following day, she was taken to Tyburn.

There, the Protestant ministers were waiting to try to persuade her to give up her faith.

She refused and prayed for a few moments. A priest was to be executed with her. He blessed her, and together they went bravely to their deaths.

Anne Line died in 1601, nearly four hundred years ago. She was declared a saint in 1970, and her feast is on 25th October.

Nicholas Owen

The house was full of strange men. Some bullied the servants in one room, and others shouted at the children in another. Two burly men in leather jerkins were pulling away wooden panelling from the walls with iron bars. Another was creeping quietly up the main wooden staircase. On each stair, he tapped, listened, tapped a second time – then moved up to the next stair, and again tapped, listened, tapped. Above him, two more men were busy with long rulers measuring heights and breadths.

Outside in the courtyard were more strange men. One stood watch over the search party's horses, and another was placed at the door of the stables. Two were poking swords into a pile of hay in a barn, shouting and laughing to each other. A fifth was even searching the pig sty. He lashed with a stick to make the pigs move, then peered deep into the darkness of their shelter.

In the main room of the house, the Great Hall, the leader of the party sat at a long table holding a goblet of wine. Behind him, one of his men squatted in the empty fireplace looking up the chimney. In front of him stood the mistress of the house.

"We know there are priests hiding here," he said to her.

"You know a great deal," she answered calmly.

"We have information."

"You are very lucky."

"We know their hiding places."

"Then you will find them quickly," she said, adding, "and you will not need to tear my house apart."

He stood up angrily, and strode from the room, shouting to his men to search harder.

And search they did. For two more days they continued to tear away panelling, to look up chimneys, to take measurements, to poke with swords, and to tap at floors and staircases listening for hollow sounds. But in all this time they found nothing. In the end they had to leave, cursing the person who had given them information, and telling the mistress that they would soon be back.

After they had gone, she sat alone in the Great Hall and waited. A servant came and asked if the hiders should be told that it was now safe to come out.

"Not yet," she answered. "We must wait until we know that the search party has really gone."

For two hours she waited. At the end of that time, one of the farmers from the nearby village came to inform her that all the horsemen had ridden away. They must be several miles from the house by this time. Only then did she stand up and, accompanied by a single servant, go through the corridors, past the broken panelling and up the damaged stairs.

At the end of one of the upstairs rooms was a closet – a large wardrobe separated off from the room by a curtain. There was no plaster on the walls inside the closet. They were made of bare brick between large, upright beams of dark wood.

The searchers had been here, of course, tapping and poking and measuring. But they had found nothing. Now the mistress pointed to one of the beams and said to the servant, "Quickly."

He placed his hands at the top of the beam and pushed. At first nothing happened. Then he pushed again. Slowly, the bottom of the beam began to move outwards. When it had moved far enough for him to put his hands round the bottom, he bent down, grasped it and lifted so that the beam stuck straight out from the wall. Having done this, he stepped to one side.

The raised beam left behind a narrow space in the bricks, just wide enough for an adult to squeeze through. It was musty and very dark. The mistress put her head into the space.

"Father," she called. "Father."

There was a noise in the darkness, and a pale face appeared in the gap. With a helping hand from the servant, the owner of the face struggled into the room. He was dressed in a priest's robes and the mistress of the house knelt before him.

"Praise God that you are safe, Father," she said.

"God working through Brother Nicholas," the priest answered.

A second man, very small and with a grizzled beard, had climbed limping out of the hiding place. He was dressed in the clothes of a carpenter, and looked strong despite his size and his limp. He, too, knelt in front of the priest to receive a blessing.

At the time of Edmund Campion and Anne Line, scenes like this were common in England and Wales. The law said that people could be Catholics if they wished and if they paid extra taxes and fines. But it was treason to be a Catholic priest, and treason to help one. So anyone wanting to be a real Catholic – to hear Mass, to be married or confirmed, to go to confession – was a traitor. And the punishment for traitors was death.

After Edmund Campion's execution, many more priests came to England. They travelled under false names celebrating Mass and hearing confessions. It was dangerous work. Spies were everywhere, and it was always possible that the hunters were close behind.

As the priest bent before the altar or raised the host, the searchers might be gathering under the trees outside – ready to come battering at the door and tearing through the house. It was at moments

A second man, very small and with a grizzled beard,
had climbed limping out of the hiding place.

like these that the priests disappeared up false chimneys, underneath staircases and into holes hidden in walls behind false beams.

Many of these hides had been built by the little man who followed the priest out of the opening in the bricks, the man the priest called Nicholas. This was Nicholas Owen, a priest's servant, a Catholic, a carpenter and one of the most wanted men in England.

Nicholas's hides were so cleverly made that the priest could disappear at a moment's warning – almost from under the searchers' noses. Sometimes priests lived in them for several days while the searchers looked.

But if the priest was to stay hidden, the hide had to be secret. Only the most trusted servants could know of it. This meant hides were very difficult to build. Nicholas could not simply start cutting away the stairs to construct a little room beneath. A spying servant might see him, or a visitor or a child. So, the little carpenter had to make the hides at night, and nearly always alone.

Often he would work all day on a building job, a new staircase or landing, or an alteration in the doors. The job was his reason for being in the house. Then, at night when all were asleep, he would take out his tools and start again, this time on the hide.

For years he continued with this work. But in 1605, a group of unhappy Catholics tried to blow up the new king and his parliament. One of them, Guy Fawkes, was arrested while he was about the task. The other members of the plot were soon rounded up as well. Within weeks they had all been executed.

But for the English Catholics that was not the end of the matter. The government wanted to get rid of all the country's priests, and hunted them down more fiercely than ever.

So, less than two months after the Gunpowder Plot, a group of armed men gathered outside Hindlip House near Worcester. There were more than a hundred of them, and their job was to find priests.

The search was like many other searches. There was a loud battering on the front door, and when it did not open, the leader ordered it to be broken down. Once inside, the men spread out through the house. They tapped and measured and tore, but to begin with they found nothing.

Then, they made their first find. It was a hide, but it was empty. The search went on – another hide, empty again.

For four days, they ransacked the house doing everything they could to find those hidden in it, and finding nothing more. It seemed that there could be no priests there. The leader of the search party, certain that this was so, went home, leaving his brother behind in charge of a smaller group of men.

The brother decided to have one last try. This time the searchers were lucky. They found two men trying to leave the house, one of them a small carpenter with a grizzled beard and a limp. The men claimed they had been working in the house, but the small one was quickly recognised. It was Nicholas Owen.

He was taken from Worcester to London, and after a spell in a different prison, put in the Tower.

He had been imprisoned twice before, and the second time, he had been tortured. The gaolers had hung him up by the wrists and left him hanging for three hours. Even then he had given nothing away. Finally, they had let him go, still not knowing who he was.

This time, though, the gaolers knew him, and they knew he was a valuable prisoner. He had built most of the hiding places in England, and he knew more about them than anyone else. He knew which houses were Catholic, where the secret Masses were said and where the priests hid. In fact, he knew almost enough to destroy Catholicism in England. And the gaolers were determined that he would tell them everything.

In those days, there were rules about the use of torture. According to these Nicholas could not be put on the rack because his health was too bad. The rules were ignored, and he was racked several times. Despite the pain, he gave no information away, and said nothing that could put other Catholics in danger. On 2nd February, he died under torture.

Nicholas Owen was declared a saint in 1970. We celebrate his feast on 25th October.